Throughout the ages seers and wise men have consulted the stars in their search to foretell the future. Their studies and learning have resulted in the creation of the body of knowledge known as Astrology. Our astrologer JO SHERIDAN has time and time again demonstrated her uncanny talents in the practice of the ancient Art. Those who come to her for advice are constantly amazed by the accuracy of her predictions and the soundness of her guidance.

Let Jo Sheridan do the same for you. Let the revered and ancient Art of Astrology foretell YOUR future in 1979.

Published by Granada Publishing Limited
in Mayflower Books 1978

ISBN 0 583 13021 6

A Mayflower Original
Copyright © Jo Sheridan 1978
Mystic Star illustration on page 24 and
The World Picture in 1979 Astrology
illustration on page 34 by Alfred Douglas
copyright © Mandragora Press 1978
Your Life in Your Hands Palmistry illustrations
on pages 26–32 by David Sheridan
copyright © Mandragora Press 1978

Granada Publishing Limited
Frogmore, St Albans, Herts AL2 2NF
and
3 Upper James Street, London W1R 4BP
1221 Avenue of the Americas, New York, NY 10020, USA
117 York Street, Sydney, NSW 2000, Australia
100 Skyway Avenue, Toronto, Ontario, Canada M9W 3A6
Trio City, Coventry Street, Johannesburg 2001, South Africa
CML Centre, Queen & Wyndham, Auckland 1, New Zealand

Made and printed in Great Britain by
Cox & Wyman Ltd, London, Reading and Fakenham
Set in Intertype Baskerville

This book is sold subject to the condition that it
shall not, by way of trade or otherwise, be lent,
re-sold, hired out or otherwise circulated
without the publisher's prior consent in any
form of binding or cover other than that in
which it is published and without a similar
condition including this condition being imposed
on the subsequent purchaser.

LEO

*

July 23–August 22

List of Contents

1	THE SUCCESS FACTOR IN YOUR HOROSCOPE: MAKE 1979 A FRUITFUL YEAR...	5
2	LUCK AROUND THE ZODIAC	19
3	THE MYSTIC STAR ANSWERS YOUR QUESTION: 'WILL MY PRESENT SITUATION SOON IMPROVE?'	23
4	YOUR LIFE IN YOUR HANDS	26
5	THE WORLD PICTURE IN 1979	33
6	YOUR PERSONAL HOROSCOPE FOR 1979	37

* 1 *

THE SUCCESS FACTOR IN YOUR HOROSCOPE: MAKE 1979 A FRUITFUL YEAR...

The date of your birth tells you which of the twelve signs of the Zodiac you belong to. Each sign has certain inborn qualities which will either help or hinder you on your pathway through life. Once you know what these are, you're better equipped to make the most of your good points and minimize the bad. This can save a lot of time and heart-ache, and guide you into activities which are likely to prove fulfilling and rewarding.

As you read through this chapter, you'll also gain a deeper understanding and awareness of the character and potential of those near and dear to you, and of the people you meet in the course of your working day.

You'll know how their minds work, how they're likely to react at the emotional level to certain situations and approaches – and you'll behave accordingly. This will inevitably sweeten your relationships, heighten your reputation as an intelligent, perceptive, sympathetic personality, and create more harmony and goodwill around you.

These are essential ingredients in the recipe for the full, rich, abundant life which we all long for. But although it's true to a certain extent to say that character is Destiny, it's also necessary for you to know the celestial pattern for the year ahead. As above, so below. Meaning that as the planets wheel through the Solar Houses high in the sky above us, making positive or negative aspects to each other, so our feelings and our fortunes here on Earth below are affected for good or ill.

So study your forecasts for the coming year which I have mapped out for you carefully, and when delays or adverse influences are shown, have patience, and exercise the arts of masterly inactivity or psychic self-defence. When it's golden opportunity time, forge ahead!

Armed with this foreknowledge, you have an excellent chance of making 1979 a happy, successful and fruitful year.

* * *

ARIES March 21–April 19

Ruling Planet: **Mars**
Symbol: **The Ram**
Element: **Fire**

Mars, god of war and passion, endows you with strength and magnetism, makes you irresistible in love and a foe to beware of.

Adventurous, courageous and independent, you're a born pioneer, destined to take the lead and blaze the trail for other, less enterprising folk to follow.

You chafe under strict supervision, resent criticism, can't abide a humdrum routine, and are happiest with an active, varied programme which gives you plenty of elbow-room and scope for using your initiative. You're in your element when you can see speedy results; brilliant at making spur-of-the-moment decisions, and capable of coping with the occasional crisis or emergency with verve and panache.

Ambitious, energetic and a fine organizer, you concentrate intently on your target, keen to get to the top in the shortest possible time, despite fierce opposition or competition. It's not the thought of more money luring you on – it's the freedom, prestige and authority of the boss position which appeals to you.

What must you guard against? You're so supremely confident you can cope with anything that comes along that you sometimes come unstuck through neglecting to take elementary safety precautions. Try to make sure that your possessions are insured to their full value, and take whatever steps are necessary to make your retirement financially secure.

You live in the present and plunge hopefully into the future – which in itself is admirable. But to go forward successfully it's sometimes necessary to go back – to retrace your footsteps and learn from the past. This is something you're rather reluctant to do, but it can be enormously worthwhile.

On reflection you may discover that throughout your life you've tended to fall into the same old traps and pitfalls through recklessness, impetuosity and impatience. If so, and if you're prepared to exercise greater self-discipline, you have it in your power to break this unsatisfactory repeat-pattern, and begin a new chapter in 1979 which is refreshingly free from such problems.

* * *

TAURUS   April 20–May 21

Ruling Planet: **Venus**
Symbol: **The Bull**
Element: **Earth**

Your Ruling Planet Venus endows you with good looks, charm and a love of beauty and harmony. Coupled with this is a practical, hard-headed approach and a flair for finance – you tend to be lucky in money matters and partnerships, and have a shrewd nose for a bargain.

That longing for power and authority which is strong in the Aries and Leo temperament is lacking in your make-up. You're attracted to well-paid positions because you adore the good things of life, and very sensibly realize that these have to be paid for.

You place a high value on security and permanence, seldom engage in anything risky or experimental, and like to build on solid foundations. Whatever you attempt, you do faithfully and well; you make sure, also, that others play their part, and measure up to your standards of excellence. Both at home and at work, you're a splendid manager, able to budget skilfully, and make the most of your resources. Dependable and discreet, you can be trusted never to betray a confidence.

At the start of the race, onlookers may be inclined to place their bets on more blatantly brilliant but less stable characters, yet members of your sign usually win through at the finish by dint of sheer persistence, determination and staying power. Your life-history is one of steady effort and achievement.

What are the drawbacks in your nature which could lessen your chances of success? You're inclined to be over-cautious at times, to get set in your ways, and cling to traditional attitudes and ways of doing things.

In the coming year, however, the celestial pattern will help you to get out of the rut, overcome your distrust of change, and open your mind to new ideas and possibilities. Fresh horizons beckon, and if you go with the flow of fortune, you'll succeed in making 1979 a happy and fruitful year.

* * *

GEMINI   May 22–June 20

Ruling Planet: **Mercury**
Symbol: **The Twins**
Element: **Air**

Your greatest asset is your speed, which is much in evidence from the moment you arrive on this planet. The Gemini baby talks, walks and learns to read and write much faster than average. With fleet-footed Mercury, messenger of the gods, on your side it's not surprising that you usually win first prize for your essay at school, and cover yourself with glory at the races!

Your ability to move with the times and latch on swiftly to new ideas stands you in good stead in business, and keeps you young at heart. Quick-thinking, friendly and persuasive, you're able to make instant contact with people of all classes and creeds, and convince them that what you're offering is worth having. Your love of travel and flair for foreign languages often takes you far from your birthplace, and you flourish abroad.

To you, variety is the spice of life. You tend to get terribly bored and your sparkle dims if you're forced to stay in the same spot too long. So you switch jobs frequently, hold down two jobs simultaneously, or have a side-line or two – or three – in addition to your main source of income. In this way, you gain lots of experience in different fields, which can be invaluable from the commercial or professional angle, and also helps to make you an interesting, entertaining raconteur.

On the other hand, your readiness to start off enthusiastically on one scheme, and then get side-tracked by something which seems more exciting and amusing, can land you in trouble. Your tendency to have too many irons in the fire, and make changes simply for the sake of change, can be costly.

The year ahead looks very promising, and if you sort out your priorities, curb your restless inclinations, and concentrate your clever mind and energies along sound, productive lines, you'll succeed in making it a truly fruitful one.

* * *

CANCER June 21–July 22

Ruling Planet: **The Moon**
Symbol: **The Crab**
Element: **Water**

There's something about you that inspires trust. People come to you with their problems and confide their deepest secrets in your sympathetic ear, knowing they'll never be repeated. Logic isn't your strong point, but you're imaginative, far-seeing and intuitive. Your first impressions, dreams and hunches often turn out to be uncannily true.

Your moods swing from elation to depression as your Ruling Planet, the Moon, waxes and wanes. Shy, sensitive, easily upset, you have a horror of scenes, and go out of your way to avoid an argument. Yet if a confrontation seems inevitable, out come your claws, and the verbal nip you inflict in self-defence can be painful.

A slow starter you may be, but you'll get there in the end, never fear! You're more ambitious than you may appear at first glance, motivated by a strong urge to win the respect of the community, and have enough cash in reserve to protect and provide for those near and dear to you.

Shrewdness, thrift and a remarkable memory aid you in your business affairs. You're also very tenacious – you hang on when those around you are collapsing in limp, exhausted little heaps. You have a lucky touch in dealing with the general public. If there's a family business or profession, you're proud to carry on the tradition.

You prize security and are devoted to home and family, but travel – especially overseas travel – exerts a powerful pull. You may live under a foreign flag for years, but will eventually return to your native land. You generally manage to save a proportion of your earnings so your retirement is free from financial cares.

Caution and a lack of confidence in certain areas can hold you back at times, but in the next twelve months Jupiter and Mars will encourage you to come out of your shell, overcome your timidity, and make 1979 a year to remember.

* * *

LEO   July 23–August 22

Ruling Planet: **The Sun**
Symbol: **The Lion**
Element: **Fire**

Of all the signs of the Zodiac yours is the one that is usually voted most likely to succeed. This doesn't depend entirely on your inborn talents, impressive though they are, or your industry. The magic of your personality also plays an important part in your triumphs. Inspired by your vitality, charm and sunny self-confidence, people flock to your banner, and are content to follow in your footsteps.

This, you feel, is just as it should be. For Leo is the Royal sign of the Zodiac, and who is better fitted to wear the crown, wield the sceptre of power, and play the leading role than yourself?

You're not afraid to take chances and have a wonderful flair for spotting and exploiting opportunities to the utmost. You concentrate on essentials, take decision-making in your stride, and carry responsibility lightly. A splendid organizer, you believe in delegating as much as possible, because you know this is the best way to get things done. Besides, it gives others a share of the limelight, and gives you more time to do the things you enjoy.

These factors, combined with your creative, visionary qualities, take you to the top of the heap in an apparently effortless fashion.

Anyone as gifted, good-looking and popular as you will inevitably arouse envy and resentment in the ranks at times. Your critics claim that you're extravagant, stubborn, domineering, and ultra-susceptible to flattery. Some or all of these things may be true, but in fairness it must also be added that you're frank, honourable and just in your dealings, free from petty jealousy and possessiveness, loyal to friends, lovers and helpers alike. There's no malice in your make-up, and you never bear a grudge.

Try to surround yourself with people who are worthy of your trust in 1979; banish yes-men and free-loaders from your realm, and you can look forward to better times ahead!

* * *

VIRGO   August 23–September 22

Ruling Planet: **Mercury**

Symbol: **The Maiden**

Element: **Earth**

Your Ruling Planet Mercury endows you with keen intelligence, a dry sense of humour, and a large bump of curiosity. You want to know how the other half lives, and make good use of any opportunity to travel. Whenever possible you choose a career that takes you abroad, and acclimatize easily to new surroundings.

You like to keep active, and are renowned for your industry, conscientiousness and reliability. But you're not overly ambitious. You have no desire to live dangerously, and are content to be the power behind the throne, letting more flamboyant characters take the lead and the limelight.

You're a perfectionist, which can be a blessing or a curse. It means that you can always be depended upon to do excellent work, and deliver on time, which is good. But to achieve this, you're inclined to drive yourself too hard, burn the candle at both ends, and wind up feeling tense, nervy and irritable. You also expect others to toe the line, and come up to your extremely high standards in all they do – which of course they don't.

You're your own toughest critic, and you're not slow either to point out the flaws and failings of others. This you do from the very best of motives, but it does tend to create difficulties both in your private and business relationships.

Try to be a little easier on yourself, and more lavish with praise and encouragement to those around you.

Despite your many excellent qualities, your progress is sometimes delayed because you dislike taking risks, hold too modest an opinion of your merits, and put your own interests last in a self-sacrificing fashion. However, it seems that the planets won't permit you to blush unseen in 1979. Whether you like it or not, you'll be dragged out of obscurity into the forefront of affairs, and there's every likelihood that you'll end the year in a more prominent, affluent position than you began it!

* * *

LIBRA   September 23–October 22

Ruling Planet: **Venus**
Symbol: **The Scales**
Element: **Air**

Your Ruling Planet Venus endows you with good looks, charm and discretion. You have a flair for pouring oil on troubled waters, reconciling those who are at loggerheads, and creating an atmosphere of peace, beauty and harmony around you.

Lean years of apprenticeship and hard slog are foreign to your luxury-loving, rather indolent temperament, but you have a fine mind and a skilful way of turning circumstances to good account. The lonely eminence of the leader's lot is not what you're aiming for. You have no burning urge to give the orders, work round the clock, and carry a heavy load of responsibility.

This is the sign of partnership, and you function best in a clean, pleasant environment, surrounded by congenial people whose experience and strength you can rely on whenever necessary.

Blessed with a sweet, gentle, amiable disposition, you don't have to strive for popularity – it lands in your lap. You have the knack of winning the affection and goodwill of your associates; influential people, too, have a tendency to smile upon you, and regard you as an asset.

Yielding and pliable as you may appear on the surface, you're still an adept at getting your own way. You handle awkward customers in a marvellously adroit, tactful fashion, and are a clever negotiator.

You're a good listener, always prepared to see and sympathize with the other person's point of view. Maybe it's this inborn ability to see all round a situation that makes it difficult for you to make decisions in a hurry. Critics condemn you for sitting on the fence when swift action is called for, and you could try getting off it occasionally in 1979.

But no one can deny that your tolerance, diplomacy and serenity are admirable qualities. If we were all as ready as you are to compromise and seek for a peaceful rather than a violent solution to problems, this battle-scarred old planet of ours might be a happier place to live on.

* * *

SCORPIO October 23–November 21

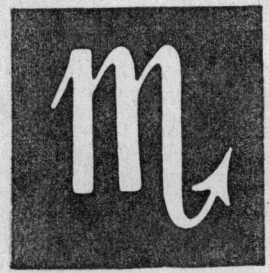

Ruling Planets: **Mars and Pluto**

Symbol: **The Scorpion**

Element: **Water**

Mars and Pluto, your Ruling Planets, endow you with dynamic energy, enthusiasm, and a fascinating, mysterious, magnetic personality. They also give you great courage and determination in the face of danger and opposition. To you, life is a battle which must be won, and you love, fight, hate and endure with all the strength and force of your passionate nature.

Yours is one of the most perceptive, probing, intuitive signs of the Zodiac, difficult to deceive, with a flair for tuning into other people's motives, and anticipating their movements with uncanny precision. But you believe that silence is power, and are usually very reserved about your own affairs. Your emotions are kept well concealed under a calm, controlled exterior, and if someone close to you betrays one of your secrets, you find it hard to forgive.

Spurred on by ambition, you have the necessary drive,

application and concentration to overcome many obstacles and achieve your goal. Money is important to you because of the authority and security that it brings, and you flourish in partnerships. Yet you're such a fierce individualist that you choose to play a lone hand whenever possible.

The independence which you prefer has several advantages – it's quicker, for instance, for you to make a decision and carry it through rather than sit around, seething inwardly, while a group of people discuss the pros and cons, and take forever to make up their minds.

But carrying the load single-handed often means that you become over-burdened, make work the mainspring of your life, and permit it to dominate your leisure hours. Over-working is one of the socially acceptable sins; it does, however, have a depleting effect on your health and spirits.

The planets are swinging in your favour in 1979, and you'll make it a joyful, fruitful year if you allow others to share some of the responsibilities, and give yourself more time for rest, relaxation and enjoyment.

* * *

SAGITTARIUS November 22–December 21

Ruling Planet: **Jupiter**
Symbol: **The Centaur**
Element: **Fire**

The arrow which the Centaur shoots from his bow is the arrow of intuition for which you are justly renowned. A highly developed sixth sense coupled with a first-class brain is a formidable combination, and many celebrated seers and financial wizards belong to your sign of the Zodiac.

Jupiter, your Ruling Planet, gives you your lucky breaks, and your cheerful, confident, optimistic outlook. It is from the jovial planet, also, that you derive your love of fair play, hearty appreciation of the good things of life, and respect for pomp, ceremony and tradition.

Your warmth, tolerance and lively sense of humour make you

immensely popular with both sexes, and your little black book is filled with interesting names and addresses. You enjoy giving and receiving hospitality, can be relied on to break the ice at any gathering, and have an inborn flair for mixing business with pleasure.

'Don't fence me in', is your theme-song. Independent, strong-willed and resourceful, you value your freedom, and like to keep on the move. The world is your oyster, and you usually flourish in far-away places.

You may appear easy-going on the surface, but underneath are the seeds of ambition. Versatile, adaptable and adventurous, you're prepared to break new ground, and explore a number of interesting possibilities in your search for what really suits you.

One of your many virtues is your readiness to take chances and cast your bread upon the waters. As your luck is proverbial, you often get it back buttered! Anything in the nature of a gamble draws you like a magnet, and you generally do well in risky, speculative ventures. You gravitate naturally to a position of power and authority, usually around middle-age, where you enjoy the sweets of success, and the respect and affection of the community.

The celestial pattern in the year ahead will suit your temperament perfectly, and you should have no difficulty whatsoever in making this an enjoyable, fruitful year.

* * *

CAPRICORN December 22–January 19

Ruling Planet: **Saturn**
Symbol: **The Mountain Goat**
Element: **Earth**

Ruled by Saturn, stern task-master of the gods, many members of your sign suffer deprivations of various kinds in childhood, but this simply acts as a spur. Deep-rooted in your nature is a strong streak of ambition, and you're a born climber. You generally achieve your goal in the end, more by dint of determination, industry and perseverance than by good luck.

Active, energetic and efficient, you plan ahead carefully; believe in setting money aside for a rainy day, may invest in something safe and solid such as property, but are reluctant to speculate. You're equally cautious where relationships are concerned. Anyone who tries to sweep you off your feet is likely to be rebuffed, but once a bond has been established, you're extremely loyal.

This is one of the signs of longevity, and you'll probably live to a ripe old age. You have lasting good looks and are usually more attractive in maturity than at seventeen.

The habit of over-working and expecting the worst is deeply ingrained in your character. Like Virgo and Scorpio, you're convinced that if you don't do the job yourself, it won't be done properly. Often this means that you drive yourself too hard, and cut yourself off from love and the lighter side of life, which is a pity.

However, in the year ahead it looks as if you won't have to struggle quite as hard as you usually do to make your mark. Virtue will be rewarded; life opens out, and you'll have some marvellous opportunities to expand your boundaries and widen your sphere of influence.

To make 1979 a really fruitful year, you must try to look on the bright side, learn to relax and rely on others a little more – and you won't be disappointed. You'll find there is much to be gained in terms of health, wealth and happiness by sharing the load, and devoting more of your time and attention to friends, loved ones and pleasurable, leisure-time activities.

* * *

AQUARIUS January 20–February 18

Ruling Planet: **Uranus**
Symbol: **The Water-Bearer**
Element: **Air**

Your Ruling Planet Uranus, the great transformer, makes you a born rebel, dissatisfied with things as they are, unwilling to conform to established attitudes and conventional behaviour patterns.

Your brilliant, inventive, original ideas make you an asset to any go-ahead organization. You move with the times (sometimes well ahead of them), and are never afraid to tackle something new and different. But as you dislike working to routine, function in fits and starts, and resent supervision, you're best running your own show.

A career that is also a calling, a vocation, suits your idealistic temperament. The feeling that you're doing something worthwhile for humanity and progress is more important to you than a high salary or security. You enjoy fighting for a cause that is dear to your heart – even a lost cause. Money and material possessions usually come low on your list of priorities, and you're not unduly bothered about how you'll fare in your twilight years.

You're different from the crowd – a constant source of fascination to a host of devoted friends and followers who delight in your stimulating company. But though you're charming, sympathetic and understanding, there's a certain air of detachment about you, and you always remain something of an enigma, even to those near and dear to you. You believe very strongly in the freedom of the individual, are refreshingly free from any taint of jealousy, and expect others to be equally unpossessive about you.

As a general rule you fight shy of close involvements, prefer to play a lone hand, and do it your way. There are times when this is advisable, but think very seriously about an alternative arrangement in 1979. Planetary trends in the coming year place a marked emphasis on togetherness at every level of your life, and you could find much happiness and satisfaction in the right partnership.

* * *

PISCES   February 19–March 20

Ruling Planets: **Jupiter and Neptune**

Symbol: **Two Fishes**

Element: **Water**

Members of your charming, lovable sign are renowned for their sensitivity, fertile imagination, uncanny sixth sense and creative, artistic flair. Neptune, planet of glamour and inspiration, will heighten and enhance these qualities during the next twelve months. This will aid you in every area of your life, and (coupled with a helping hand from Jupiter, your kindly co-Ruler), should have a particularly uplifting effect on your occupational affairs.

One of your greatest strengths is your adaptability. You can adjust easily to other people's moods, take an interest in what interests them, mix in any society, and fit into almost any kind of job – provided it's not a monotonous dead-ender.

Carping critics may complain that you prefer pleasure to work. Could it be that they envy your marvellous capacity for carefree enjoyment of the good things in life? They also mutter darkly about your extravagance and reckless generosity, but you're born lucky where windfalls, gambling and speculative ventures are concerned, so this evens up the score to some extent.

Your Zodiacal symbol, two fishes tied together with a silver cord, swimming in opposite directions, reveals inner conflict. All too often you're torn between conflicting desires and loyalties; can't decide which choice to make, or which path to follow. In such situations, your best policy is to ask for advice from someone sensible who has no axe to grind – and heed it. Remember that the onlooker sees most of the game, and can view your dilemma with the necessary detachment.

Tender-hearted and compassionate, you're always very willing – too willing sometimes – to help lame dogs over styles. Some members of the breed who approach you in 1979 will be genuine, but others will be time-wasting phonies, out to take advantage of your good nature. You're endearingly eager to see only the nicest side, and ignore the faults and failings of others, but do try to be more selective and discriminating, and in this way you'll ensure that you have a year of real progress and prosperity!

* * *

* 2 *

LUCK AROUND THE ZODIAC

Have you a fond attachment for a certain item of clothing which is far from new, but which you keep on wearing on special occasions because you feel it's lucky to you?

Chances are there's a link between the happy, confident, fortunate feeling it gives you and its colour. This colour in turn is linked to the planet which holds dominion over your sign of the Zodiac.

A centuries-old tradition tells us that each of the planets has its own set of 'correspondences' – colours, numbers, days, jewels and flowers – which are believed to attract good vibrations, and regarded as bringers of good fortune.

Why this should be so is a mystery which may be unravelled in our life-time. Thanks to the splendid work of psychic and scientific researchers, our knowledge and understanding of the finer forces and invisible influences is increasing, and many beliefs which were formerly dismissed as mere superstition are now seen to be valid.

Meanwhile, as we can all do with a little bit of extra luck, here is a list of your luck-bringers, which you can try out and test for yourself.

* * *

ARIES: Your life unfolds in 9-year-cycles. 9 is your lucky number, Tuesday your lucky day. To attract good vibrations you should wear and have around you the colours red and mustard yellow. Your lucky jewel is the blood-stone, emblem of courage and charm against ills and accidents. It is said to bring renown, favours and distinctions to the wearer. The honeysuckle, signifying 'bonds of love', is your fortunate flower.

* * *

TAURUS: Your life unfolds in 6-year-cycles. 6 is your lucky number, Friday your lucky day. To attract good vibrations you should wear and have around you all shades of blue and pastel pinks. Your birth-stone is the turquoise, an emblem of love and healing. It is said to protect the wearer against falls, headaches and the evil eye. The red rose, signifying 'pleasure and passion', is your fortunate flower.

* * *

GEMINI: Your life unfolds in 5-year-cycles. 5 is your lucky number, Wednesday your lucky day. To attract good vibrations you should wear and have around you pale yellows and silver-greys. Your birth-stone is the topaz, an emblem of health and strength. It is said to bring peace of mind and prosperity, and is particularly helpful to the traveller and job-hunter. The iris, meaning 'message and enlightenment', is your fortunate flower.

* * *

CANCER: Your life unfolds in 7-year-cycles. 2 and 7 are your lucky numbers, Monday your lucky day. To attract good vibrations you should wear and have around you sea-green, silver and white. Your birth-stone is the pearl, an emblem of radiance, purity and truth. It is said to have the power to cool fevers, attract true love and loyal friends. Your fortunate flower is honesty, also known as Lunary, signifying sincerity, foresight and money-luck.

* * *

LEO: Your life unfolds in 10-year-cycles. The 40's and 60's are peak periods. Your lucky number is 1, lucky day Sunday. To attract good vibrations you should wear and have around you flame-yellow, orange and gold. Your birth-stone is the diamond, an emblem of joy, wisdom and illumination; a charm against danger, and a strengthener of the bonds of love and friendship. The Sunflower, signifying 'pride and riches', is your fortunate flower.

* * *

VIRGO: Your life unfolds in 5-year-cycles. 5 is your lucky number, Wednesday your lucky day. To attract good vibrations you should wear and have around you pale yellows, light greys and fawns. Your birth-stone is the aquamarine, an emblem of youth, hope and integrity. It ensures a safe journey, and is said to keep married love fresh and blooming. Rosemary, signifying 'always in my thoughts', is your fortunate flower.

* * *

LIBRA: Your life unfolds in 6-year-cycles; peak periods are from twenty-four to thirty, and forty-two to forty-eight. Your lucky number is 6, Friday your lucky day. To attract good vibrations you should wear and have around you delicate greens, pastel blues and pinks. Your birth-stone is the sapphire, an emblem of enlightenment and discretion. It ensures constancy in love, and protects the wearer against ill-wishing. The white rose, signifying 'idealistic love', is your fortunate flower.

* * *

SCORPIO: Your life unfolds in 9-year-cycles. 9 is your lucky number, Tuesday your lucky day. To attract good vibrations you should wear and have around you red and lime-yellow. Your birth-stone is the garnet, symbolizing 'light in darkness'. It is reputed to have the power to banish grief, arouse love and increase the popularity and prosperity of the wearer. The lesser celandine, which means 'joys to come', is your fortunate flower.

* * *

SAGITTARIUS: Your life unfolds in 3-year-cycles; the thirtieth birthday is particularly eventful. 3 is your lucky number, Thursday your lucky day. To attract good vibrations you should wear and have around you shades of violet, rich blues, purple and wine. Your birth-stone is the amethyst, an emblem of truth, benevolence and dignity. It guards the wearer against temptation, and attracts success in financial affairs. Purple lilac, signifying 'profit and expansion after difficulties', is your fortunate flower.

* * *

CAPRICORN: Your life unfolds in 8-year-cycles. 8 is your lucky number, Saturday your lucky day. To attract good vibrations you should wear and have around you shades of green, brown and black. Your birth-stone is the ruby, an emblem of cheerfulness and durability. It preserves health and beauty, attracts and keeps love and friendship, secures possessions to their rightful owner. The snowdrop, signifying 'hope and consolation', is your fortunate flower.

* * *

AQUARIUS: Your life unfolds in alternate 4- and 10-year-cycles. 4 is your lucky number, Saturday your lucky day. To attract good vibrations you should wear and have around you peacock blue and green. Your birth-stone is amber, a magical love-talisman, believed to increase the fascination of the wearer. It is also regarded as a general health preserver and safeguard against infection. The crocus, meaning 'hope springs anew', is your fortunate flower.

* * *

PISCES: Your life unfolds in alternate 3- and 7-year-cycles. 3 and 7 are your lucky numbers, Thursday your lucky day. To attract good vibrations you should wear and have around you sea-green, purple and mauve. Your birth-stone is the emerald, an emblem of faith, hope and courage. It is said to be good for the eyesight; bestows love, eloquence, distinctions and a knowledge of hidden and future events. The modest violet, signifying 'I return your love', is your fortunate flower.

* * *

* 3 *

THE MYSTIC STAR ANSWERS YOUR QUESTION: 'WILL MY PRESENT SITUATION SOON IMPROVE?'

This old but ever-new method of forecasting the future for yourself is quite simple to work, and demands no complex calculations. According to magical lore and legend, the accuracy of the answer received depends greatly on the sincerity of the querent.

If you're truly concerned about your present situation, and you really do want to know the answer to the question, the answer you invoke will be relevant, and you'll probably find that it's amazingly accurate.

And now let's begin! Place the Mystic Star Map on page 24 on a firm, flat surface, with the angle containing Star Number 3 facing towards the East.

Then close your eyes, raise your right hand above the Mystic Star, trace an imaginary eight-pointed star in the air with your index finger, and say the following words:

> 'Star bright, star light
> Tell me true, tell me right
> Will my present situation soon improve?'

You may utter these words aloud, or say them inwardly, just as you please.

After a moment or two devoted to visualizing the improvements you would like to take place, point your index finger downwards and lower it until it touches the surface of the Map. Open your eyes and check on the number of the Star you have touched.

If your finger-tip is resting on Star Number 5, for example, look up the List of Answers and you will discover *your* answer: 'Good fortune is swiftly approaching.'

This should raise your spirits immediately. But what if you discover that your finger-tip has landed on one of the vacant spaces between the Stars, or outside the outline of the Mystic Star Map?

This in itself is a message from the Oracle that the moment of inquiry was not auspicious, and you must seek again for enlightenment, but not until at least twenty-four hours have passed.

Instead of using your finger-tip as a pointer to a Star you may, if you wish, use a pin, a pencil, a cocktail stick or any other suitable wand-shaped object. This is very much a matter of personal taste.

Some of my readers tell me that they prefer to choose a quiet moment, when they're alone and unlikely to be interrupted, to consult the Oracle. This, they believe, heightens their powers of concentration and invocation. Others claim that they get equally accurate answers when they form a magic circle with a group of friends.

If you want to be a popular party-giver, you'll find it helps a lot to provide your guests with the Mystic Star Map and List of Answers. I promise you this will act as a kind of magical ice-breaker, and there won't be a dull moment. People of all ages, from all walks of life, will mingle happily together, united by the desire which burns in every human heart to see into the future, and find the right answer!

The Mystic Star

List of Answers according to the Numbers on the Stars:

1. Influential friends will assist.
2. Not if a certain party can prevent it.
3. You have much to look forward to.
4. The worst is over. Patience!
5. Good fortune is swiftly approaching.
6. Provided you permit no interference with your plans.
7. If you are prepared to take a chance.
8. No. The time is not yet ripe.
9. There are as yet many obstacles to overcome.
10. A little, soon. A lot, later.
11. Yes, but don't rest on your oars until you're safely out of troubled waters.
12. Resign yourself to some little delay in the matter.
13. It may be worse before it is better.
14. At a time when you least expect it.
15. When the wish turns into the will, hope flies in by the window-sill.

* 4 *

YOUR LIFE IN YOUR HANDS

Look at the Map of the Hand and you'll discover that the Life-line encircles the fleshy pad at the root of the thumb which is called the Mount of Venus. (*Fig. 1.*)

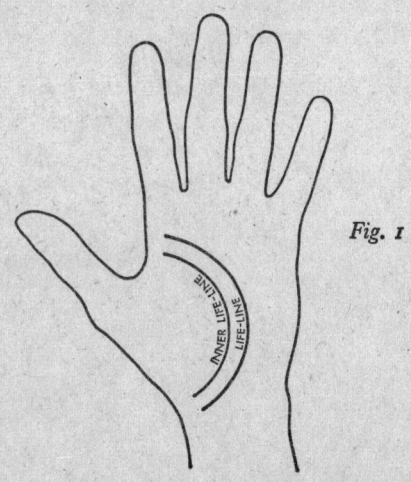

Fig. 1

The Life-line is an indication of your health and vitality. When it is long, clear and unbroken this suggests that you're robust and destined to live to a ripe old age.

If it is short or broken, don't jump to the dire conclusion that your life-span will be short. Examine the thumb. If it is strong and has a long, well-shaped nail section this indicates strong will-power; you'll hold on to life with dogged determination.

The appearance of the Inner Life-line – a completely separate line running parallel to the Life-line within the Mount of Venus – is also a great strengthener. It is a happy portent of resistance to the perils and ills that afflict mankind. (*Fig. 2.*)

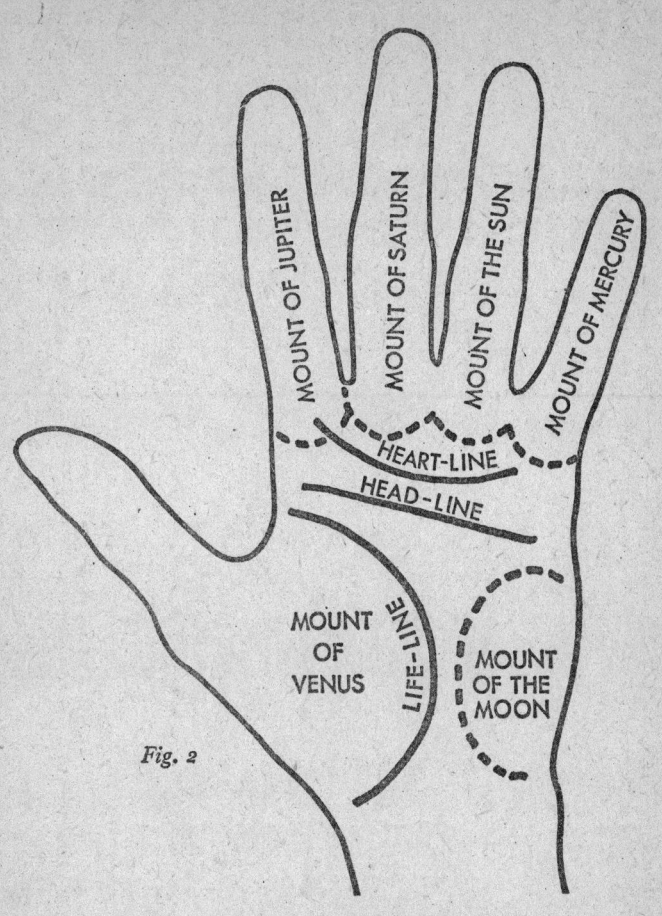

The Map of the Hand

Here you see the Life-line, the Head-line and the Heart-line. The fleshy pads at the root of the fingers, starting with the index finger, are called the Mount of Jupiter, the Mount of Saturn, the Mount of the Sun and the Mount of Mercury. The Mount of Venus is encircled by the Life-line, and facing this is the Mount of the Moon.

The shape of the Life-line is important. When it is generously curved, which means that the Mount of Venus is accordingly broad and rounded, this reveals good health and a loving, sympathetic disposition. The sexual drive is strong. A love of beauty, tasteful surroundings, children and tuneful music is shown.

You may expect the contrary when the curve of the Life-line is less pronounced, and the Mount of Venus is consequently rather narrow. The owner is lacking in sex appeal and indifferent to desire. The constitution is likely to be fragile and the supply of energy limited.

Where does your Life-line begin? The point where it starts gives a valuable clue to your temperament.

Usually it starts *under* the Mount of Jupiter, but you'll sometimes come across a Life-line which begins higher up, on the Mount of Jupiter itself. This means that the owner is ambitious and lucky – a combination which is sure to lead to success of a high order. (*Fig. 3*.)

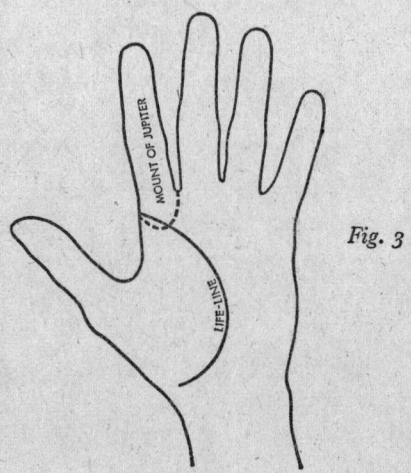

Fig. 3

A Life-line with the usual starting-point which has a branch-line running up to the Mount of Jupiter has much the same significance – it points to a self-confident, ambitious temperament and is a lucky forecast of success. (*Fig. 4*.)

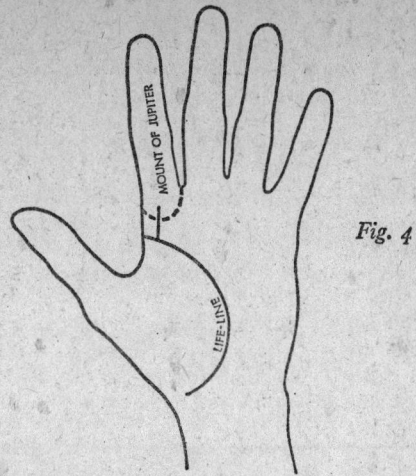

Fig. 4

A branch-line from the Life-line to the Mount of Saturn means that the harder you work the luckier you'll be. Nothing comes easy, and you may have to struggle through the school of hard knocks before you reach your goal. (*Fig. 5*.)

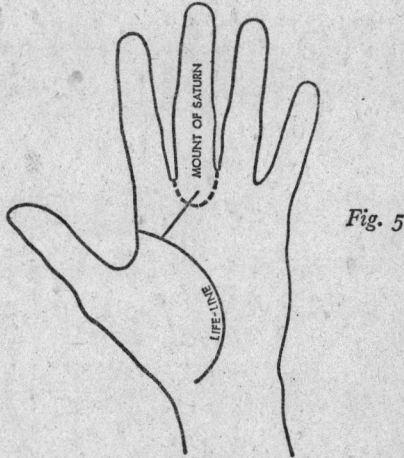

Fig. 5

A very different story is revealed if two little branch-lines run up from the beginning of the Life-line to the Head-line. This means that the person concerned is sure to get a good start in life, and can also look forward to receiving a legacy from family sources. (*Fig. 6.*)

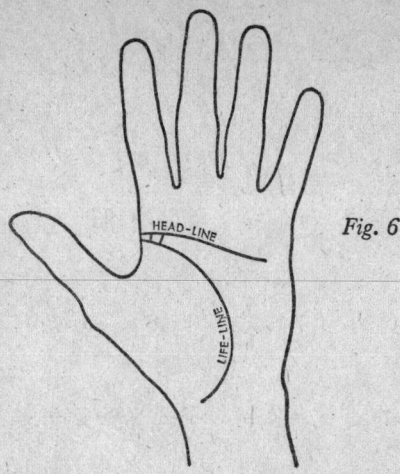

Fig. 6

A branch-line running up from the Life-line to the Mount of the Sun means that the owner's special skills and talents will be recognized and rewarded. This 'branch-line of fame' is often seen in the hands of public favourites such as actors, singers and artists. (*Fig. 7.*)

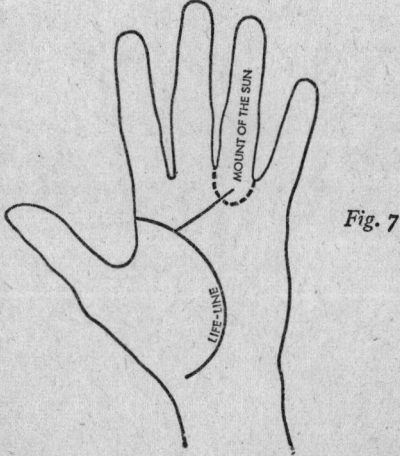

Fig. 7

The Life-line which ends in a fork with one prong curving across the hand to the Mount of the Moon indicates overseas travel. Far-off places could be your Fate. (*Fig. 8.*)

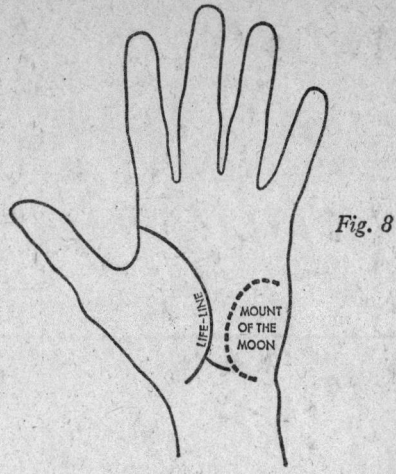

Fig. 8

The Life-line which begins by just touching the head-line shows good sense, prudence and moderation. (*Fig. 9.*)

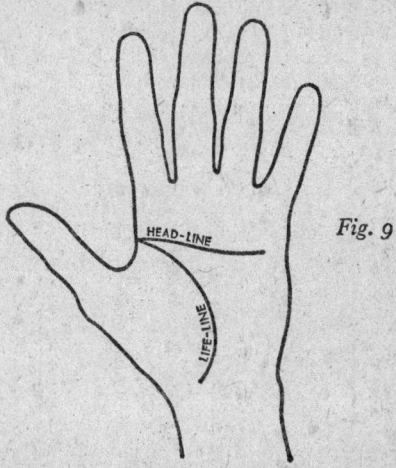

Fig. 9

When the Life-line is 'tied' to the Head-line (they start together and stay together for a while), this signifies that you lack confidence, are inclined to be over-cautious and find it hard to make decisions. You're easily hurt but praise and appreciation will work wonders for you. (*Fig. 10.*)

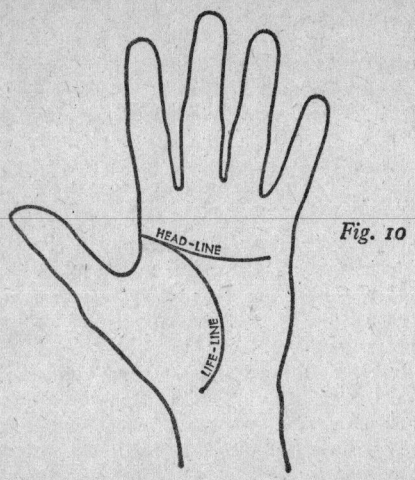

Fig. 10

A wide space between the start of the Life-line and the Head-line shows courage to the point of recklessness. Restlessness can be a problem if you're forced to lead a routine, humdrum existence, but when an emergency or crisis arises, you cope wonderfully well. You also have the courage of your own convictions, and will always speak out boldly against injustice.

* * *

* You'd like to know more about Palmistry? Read Jo Sheridan's fascinating, generously illustrated book *What Your Hands Reveal*, published by Mayflower Books in paperback at 35p.

* 5 *

THE WORLD PICTURE IN 1979

Economically the general outlook for the West appears brighter than it has done for some time. It would be too much to hope that 1979 will be a boom year, but there's certainly an encouraging indication that the world recession will be steadily counteracted, and from mid-May onwards a gradual, all-round increase in confidence should be noticeable.

International anxiety over long-term resources will be vigorously expressed as the year begins. Clashes over the planned expansion of nuclear power stations will continue to hit the headlines, and further details of past accidents which emerge will add to public unease. Despite this, more governments will decide in favour of bigger nuclear programmes on the grounds that other methods of generating power cannot do more than supplement the world's future needs.

Expanding interest in renewable, non-polluting wind, wave and solar power, however, will result in funds being allocated to further research, and the formation of an international agency to pool efforts and data may be announced.

Concern over the increase in desert areas – the unfortunate, inevitable outcome of mankind's over-use of natural resources – will result in efforts being made to limit the cutting down of trees and the wasteful clearing of vegetation.

A major scandal associated with the misuse of oil revenues may be revealed around June/July, and the activities of multinational companies in Third World countries could have political repercussions around the same time.

Britain's balance of payments situation will benefit from her new status as an oil exporter, as expected, and although the British economy will not become stable until the mid-1980s, a general improvement will become more and more apparent as the months go by.

Financial restrictions at home will still cause difficulties in the social services, particularly in regard to health and education. A rapid improvement cannot be anticipated. On the industrial relations front, an unruly start to the year will be followed by an acceptance of further curbs to check inflation, but not until after May.

Changes in law are likely to make it more attractive for owners of national treasures to retain them, and a major restructuring of the taxation system aimed at restoring incentive to workers and the self-employed could get under way in the late Spring.

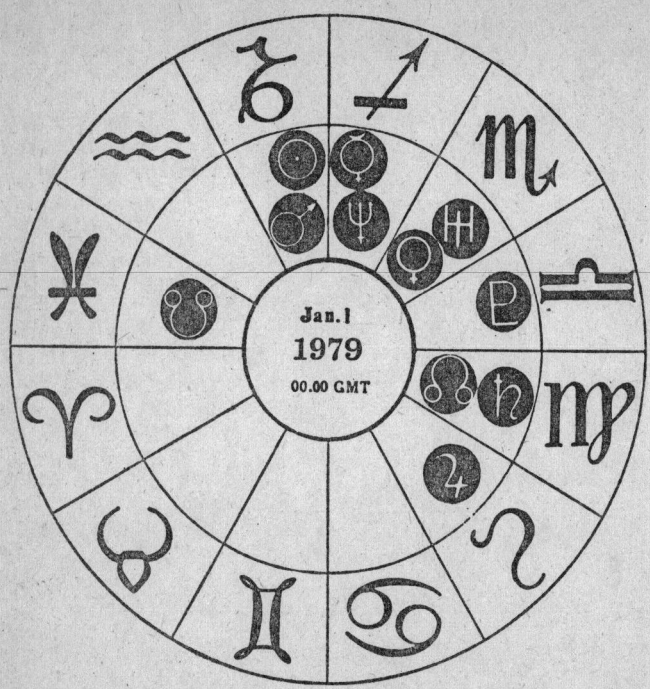

The above Horoscope shows the moment of transition from 1978 to 1979. My global predictions for the year ahead are based on the interactions between this and other significant Horoscopes.

Prices of some imported foodstuffs will soar between late February and the end of July, but other goods which became more expensive during 1977 and 1978 should drop in price from March onwards.

1979 promises to be a more satisfactory year for exports, although labour problems could be a delaying factor in the first six months. The most auspicious time for an export drive would be from the beginning of September until the end of December.

The planetary picture relating to international affairs suggests that prospects for progress towards world peace are fairly good, although policy conflicts among Soviet leaders might slow down the debate while fresh strategies are worked out. A new era of confrontation between East and West is unlikely to dawn in the year ahead.

The United States comes under generally auspicious stars, especially in the sphere of overseas affairs. Both economically and politically, America's fortunes are taking an upward trend which will strengthen the West generally.

On the domestic front, the rate of inflation should slow and unemployment figures improve after late July. Massive investment in long-term projects can be anticipated from mid-May onwards. Federal plans for urban renewal should get the go-ahead despite some powerful opposition.

Fundamental differences between the Soviet Union and Western Communist parties will not be resolved or patched over in the coming year. The Italian, French and Spanish parties especially will identify themselves more strongly with the established democratic traditions of their countries. At the same time, there are indications that the governments of Russia and France will draw closer together in matters of trade and diplomacy.

Some Eastern European states will work hard to keep the human rights issue alive and kicking, regardless of the apparent willingness of the West to compromise in favour of gains in other areas.

Italian affairs generally will not proceed smoothly in 1979, neither in politics – where the fortunes of the left come under auspicious stars – nor in religion, where the Church may be weakened by further internal dissent. Dubious financial dealings linked with Italian seats of power will not help matters. Profound differences in matters of faith will remain unresolved while current trends prevail; we are unlikely to see a reunited Church in 1979.

To a great extent the outlook for the Middle East is very much the mixture as before. Some changes in the balance of power are forecast: Egypt's internal problems will reduce her effectiveness on the international scene, while Saudi Arabia looks all set to play a more dominant role in world affairs. Long-term influences may incline the Arab states towards more sympathetic co-operation with the West.

China's star is on the ascent now, and she may adopt a more aggressive stance towards the rest of the world. Increased political stability at home and a greater reliance on foreign expertise and technology will tie her more firmly to the world economy.

Competition between the Chinese and Russians for influence among Asian and African nations could lead to an outright confrontation in the Autumn, while China's desire to reach an understanding with India may motivate her to make concessions on the future of Tibet.

1979 will see the beginning of a period of major changes for Japan. Old links will give way in favour of new alliances, whilst at home pressure from the left and minority groups will result in a widespread questioning of established opinion. The whole of South East Asia comes under troubled stars during the year ahead – Thailand and Korea being particularly vulnerable to unrest.

* LEO *

YOUR PERSONAL HOROSCOPE FOR 1979

JANUARY

News which arrives as the New Year bells ring out will put you in a cheerful, optimistic mood, and good fortune attends you where romance, marriage and money are concerned.

Happy reunions and pleasantly surprising happenings in regard to home and family affairs are forecast on the 3rd, the 4th, the 22nd and the 31st. Gains and benefits come to you in roundabout ways; someone close to you will enjoy an unexpected stroke of luck in which you will share, and you may also receive a tangible token of appreciation – a belated Christmas gift, perhaps – from a devoted admirer.

Sweet vibrations from Venus from the 7th onwards will enhance your charms, lend fresh sparkle to the social scene, and ensure that love affairs which develop during this star-blessed phase will lead to marriage and increasing prosperity before long.

Children will be a source of pride and joy to Leo parents and teachers, and the outlook is distinctly rosy for those who are eager to start a family or add to their brood.

Creative and artistic projects flourish. Many members of your sign who are intent on making their mark in the world of entertainment will win greater recognition and acclaim. A spare-time hobby or occupation may become a money-spinner, thanks to an alliance with people of similar tastes and temperament.

The 13th and the 26th are particularly significant and promising dates in regard to these matters.

Warning! Negative influences rule on the 24th, the 25th and the 30th. You're advised to keep out of arguments, hang on tight to your cash, and avoid making any important decisions or binding arrangements on these dates.

FEBRUARY *LEO*

Listen carefully to any messages, bright ideas or propositions that are made to you this month. Chance encounters or a casual conversation could introduce you to a more satisfying, independent way of making money, or get you actively involved in some new and absorbing interest.

The presence of Venus in your Solar Sixth House from the 5th onwards will lighten the load, bring you luck in occupational affairs, and surround you for the most part with an aura of harmony, co-operation and goodwill. There'll be plenty of scope for exercising your celebrated flair for organization, and you'll probably find that you can introduce some changes which will be warmly welcomed by all concerned.

Wise guidance from an older, experienced well-wisher on the 15th will encourage you to make the most of your assets, and safeguard your future. If you're in business, or fighting for a cause that is dear to your heart, dynamic vibrations from Mars will bring you the enthusiastic backing and support of powerful allies.

Thrilling developments in your love-life are forecast on this date and also on the 23rd. The arrival of an attractive newcomer will brighten your daily routine, and romance flowers in a working environment.

If a certain relationship has become increasingly strained over the past few weeks, a showdown on the 16th will clear the air considerably. Someone's absence or departure on the 26th is likely to have an advantageous outcome for you. Once again, the element of the unexpected is strong in your Destiny, and you may have a few pleasant surprises in the shape of a windfall, a bonus, a government grant or a tax rebate!

MARCH *LEO*

Throughout March and most of April Jupiter is voyaging through your Solar Twelfth House, which means that help given and received during this time will exercise a strong influence on your affairs. In a quiet, unobtrusive but very effective fashion you'll succeed in comforting and cheering those who are ill or in difficulties, and you in turn will be greatly aided by developments which are taking shape behind the scenes.

A powerful undercurrent of good luck will protect your interests, and prospects improve for your partner or spouse. Confidential information received will strengthen your hand; valuable insights will be gained, and private concerns, hush-hush negotiations and transactions flourish abundantly.

The 9th, the 20th, the 29th and the 31st are particularly significant and eventful dates in regard to these matters.

Meanwhile, the gentle presence of Venus in your Solar Seventh House from the 3rd onwards forecasts a bumper crop of Leo love affairs and weddings! Romance with a foreign, exotic flavour is much to the fore on the 5th; an invitation or a short journey on the 19th could lead to fateful meetings or reunions. The 21st and the 25th also look extremely glamorous, but you're advised to walk warily on these dates, as your popularity may arouse resentment or rivalry from an unexpected quarter.

The planetary pattern between the 4th and the 14th is fine for laying the groundwork for long-term plans, sorting out tricky legal questions, and dealing with in-laws or prospective in-laws. Overseas travel, commerce and communications from afar are also favourably aspected. In the second fortnight, however, when Mercury goes retrograde, you may expect to encounter some minor hang-ups or delays in these areas.

APRIL — *LEO*

Correspondence and discussions regarding joint funds and business ventures may require careful handling on the 2nd and the 4th. Don't be tempted to take any chances on these dates when turbulent influences are in force. Try to reassess the situation calmly; concentrate on consolidating your assets, and maintaining the peace.

After this tense, argumentative start to the month, a general, all-round improvement sets in. The 6th, the 14th and the 17th are excellent for dealing with accounts, insurance and income-tax matters. You may discover, to your relief, that you're entitled to some allowances, benefits or grants which you hadn't previously reckoned on. Gains and goodies arrive by a secret route, and those who are in line for a legal settlement or a legacy may hear something to their advantage.

Daring new projects, overseas travel and foreign affairs are favourably aspected, and lively, progressive happenings are forecast on the 10th, the 23rd and the 24th. Fresh horizons beckon, and many Leos will decide to up sticks and try their luck abroad. An offer or an invitation from a distance may take you far from familiar territory; lasting links and alliances will be forged with someone from another country, and romance blossoms under strange skies.

The period between the 12th and the 14th is highlighted by enjoyable outings, visits and get-togethers. News of a birth, forthcoming wedding, or an unexpected meeting with an old friend or an old flame will provide cause for rejoicing and merry-making.

Jupiter moves back into Leo again on the 20th, marking the beginning of a tremendously expansive phase in your life. More about this next month!

MAY   *LEO*

Jupiter is now firmly entrenched in your sign, and will remain there until the end of September. During this lucky five-month cycle you stand to benefit greatly through the goodwill, generosity and good fortune of people closely connected with you. Plans launched about a year ago will come to fruition, speculative ventures prosper, and this should establish you in a much more solvent situation.

Romantic affairs, pleasurable pursuits and creative, artistic interests also come under this planet's expansive, protective, convivial sway, and before the year is out many of your fondest wishes will be realized.

All-in-all, you'll enjoy more than your usual share of the good things in life, which will be very pleasant. The only snag is that you may have some difficulty in keeping your elegant waistline, so watch it!

Meanwhile, that starry emphasis on travel and overseas affairs persists, and stirring developments are forecast on the 3rd and the 9th. In general, major changes in the months ahead will work out splendidly for adventurous Leos who are thinking of going abroad, either on a temporary or a permanent basis.

Any lengthy frustrations or delays in regard to finance and property matters should come to an end on the 10th. This date also marks the entry of Mercury into your Solar Tenth House – a lucky omen for those who are arranging interviews and conferences in connection with their work.

Mercury is joined by Mars on the 16th, and Venus follows suit on the 18th; this powerful combination of planetary forces will put you on easy terms with wealthy, influential folk. Business-cum-pleasure occasions will produce golden dividends, and you'll forge ahead rapidly.

JUNE *LEO*

An eventful, strenuous but very rewarding month ahead! Energizing Mars is blazing across the mid-Heaven of your horoscope, focusing attention on your worldly aims and ambitions, enhancing your magnetism and giving you the drive and determination to overcome any obstacles that stand between you and your chosen goals.

Glamorize your image, circulate as much as possible, and make your wishes and intentions known in the right quarters. Good vibrations from Venus will ease your upward path, and ensure that your special qualities are noticed and appreciated by those who count in your scheme of things. New business enterprises can be launched successfully; friendly alliances, speculative ventures and community projects are brilliantly aspected, and a swift rise in your stock, status and income is indicated.

People you meet both at work and during your leisure hours will be warmly responsive to your ideas and suggestions, and you'll be greatly sought after. Fresh vistas open up, romance beckons, and prospects are particularly rosy for Leos whose loving attachments and career interests are entwined.

The 12th, the 27th and the 29th are particularly significant and fortunate dates in regard to the above matters.

Be warned, however, that clashes between home and outside interests are liable to crop up on the 1st and the 8th. Tact and diplomacy on your part will be required to keep everybody happy. You're also advised to keep love and friendship in separate compartments on the 4th, the 10th and the 28th.

Star-trends prevailing on the 18th, the 22nd and the 24th favour your private affairs, investigations and studies. New light will be cast on an old problem; discreet property deals and domestic arrangements flourish.

JULY   *LEO*

Star-trends prevailing this month will lift you out of the rut, give your personality a special sparkle, and encourage you to set about making certain changes, alterations and reforms that are long overdue.

Good vibrations from Mercury will make it easy for you to get your message across convincingly, and luck is linked with the written, spoken or printed word on the 7th and the 11th. These are excellent dates for exchanging ideas with lively-minded people, exploring profitable side-lines, adding a new string to your bow, and exploiting to the full talents that have lain dormant or neglected.

Much fruitful, enjoyable activity is indicated in connection with clubs, groups, circles, and friendly associations, particularly on the 15th and the 16th. If you're involved in social work, a community project or some other worthy cause, you'll win the respect and admiration of people in high places, and work miracles where fund-raising is concerned. Favours will be granted, hopes will be realized, and objectives you've been striving towards will be achieved in record time with the help and co-operation of enthusiastic, enterprising well-wishers.

An air of mystery and enchantment surrounds your romantic affairs, and blissful interludes are foretold around mid-month, on the 18th and the 23rd. Developments of a private, confidential nature are also indicated on the 9th and the 22nd in regard to property matters and domestic concerns which will lead to lasting benefits.

However, last month's warning about keeping friendship and love apart is repeated on the 21st, when adverse stars are in force. Make safety-first your motto, and avoid anything shady or clandestine on this date.

AUGUST *LEO*

This promises to be one of the peak months of 1979! An extraordinary concentration of planets in your sign will bring you luck and give you a fresh lease of life and vitality. Both mentally and physically you'll be at your brightest and best. Your warmth, wit and beguiling ways will make you the centre of attention, and wherever you go you'll attract a host of new friends and ardent admirers to your side.

Travel, adventure and romance are star-blessed, and thrilling developments are forecast on the 3rd, the 11th, at mid-month and later on the 27th and the 30th.

If you're engaged in creative, artistic pursuits, these dates are also likely to produce some satisfying results and a heartening burst of applause. Sports, gambling and speculative ventures pay off handsomely.

Those involved in sea-going activities, in wines, spirits, oils, chemicals, the glamour professions and the film industry should do spectacularly well, provided they act quickly.

Marked progress will be made in matters which come into the private and confidential category on the 9th and the 19th. These may be connected with real estate, a change of address or the improvement and rearrangement of your present premises. Some secret opposition or rivalry may be unmasked a week later, but you'll be able to deal with this firmly and effectively, and a happy outcome is predicted on the 28th.

Warning! Dangerous aspects are operating on the 26th, so don't jump to any rash conclusions, don't sign any important papers, and exercise special care if you're looking after youngsters or handling electrical equipment in the home on this date. Double-check travel schedules, and drive cautiously.

SEPTEMBER *LEO*

Venus, in addition to her amorous connotations, is also the planet of money-luck. As the month begins she is voyaging through your Solar Second House, accompanied by Mercury and your Ruling Planet, the Sun. This triple influence will swiftly put an end to various restricting and limiting circumstances, and there'll be opportunities galore to boost your financial reserves, and add to your prized possessions.

Old Saturn favours long-term plans, security measures and retirement schemes. Gains through secret channels, gifts, a legacy or a lucky win are forecast; spare-time interests and home-based occupations should also yield a rich harvest.

If you're intent on making alterations and improvements to your present abode, or hoping to move to a new address, help will arrive from an unexpected quarter, and the necessary funds will be forthcoming to foot the bills.

The 2nd, the 10th, the 17th and the 25th are starred for success and satisfaction in these matters. But mind how you go on the 7th, the 14th, and the 16th when deceptive star-trends prevail and you could easily be misled. Be sure to seek expert advice if you're in any doubt about signing important papers or contracts on these dates.

Venus and Mars combine to bless both your love and money interests on the 9th. A passionate rendezvous with someone special in some secluded nook will make your heart beat faster! There's a starry emphasis, too, on romance, enjoyable outings, visits and get-togethers on the 22nd, the 23rd and the 27th. Exciting things are happening in the lives of relatives and close associates, and there'll be great rejoicing over an engagement, a wedding, or the arrival of a little stranger.

OCTOBER   *LEO*

Jupiter is now settling comfortably into your Solar Second House, and will remain there until October 1980. This means that during the next twelve months you should see a vast improvement in your financial and material affairs.

If you've invested time and money in some special project, you'll soon begin to enjoy some substantial returns. Past efforts will be rewarded, present enterprises flourish and expand, and golden opportunities to branch out along new paths will land in your lap.

You'll be able to mix business with pleasure advantageously, and closer links will be forged with wealthy, influential people who are ready and willing to advance your interests. In some cases, a friendly or romantic attachment with a cheerful, generous, perceptive person whom you meet on a business or professional basis will take you into a higher income bracket.

Meanwhile from the 7th onwards the planetary pattern favours home and domestic concerns, and pleasantly surprising happenings are forecast on the 20th, and 23rd and the 27th.

Mars is thrusting through your sign throughout the month, presenting you with fresh challenges, helping you to make energetic inroads on tasks that have previously seemed too difficult to tackle, and encouraging you to be pretty ruthless if need be in banishing any irksome or depleting elements from your life.

There may be a few heated arguments or confrontations around mid-month and later, on the 25th and the 31st, but don't let this stop you from doing what you know is right. The reins of power are in your own capable hands, and if you take the initiative and force the pace a bit, great things will be accomplished.

NOVEMBER *LEO*

Harmony and goodwill surround you as the month begins. Good companions rally round, and family gatherings on the 1st and the 16th will be pleasant and enjoyable. The fortunes of those near and dear to you are on the up-swing; your partner or spouse may have exciting news to relate of a long-awaited promotion or increase in assets.

Foreign affairs are much to the fore on the 2nd and the 30th. A loving message from across water will please you, and journeys end in happy re-unions.

The 3rd and the 4th are splendid days for career-minded Leos. Some ambitious project will reach a successful climax, and celebrations and congratulations are in order!

The social whirl looks inviting; you'll occupy the centre of the stage, and there'll be no lack of ardent applicants for your favours. The 20th, the 21st and the 26th are glamorous days when dreams come true, and romance, pleasurable pastimes and entertaining are brilliantly starred. If you're tempted to stray along the primrose path of dalliance at any time, try to behave very discreetly lest you upset someone's feelings.

These three last-mentioned dates are also extremely lucky for games of chance, gambling, speculative ventures and creative, artistic interests. But watch your step on the 5th, the 24th and the 25th, when extravagance and recklessness could be your undoing.

For the most part, domestic concerns continue to prosper, particularly on the 17th, the 19th and the 28th. A few minor delays or complications are liable to occur in certain areas from the 18th onwards, when Mercury is in retrograde motion, but this should all be cleared up completely by the 29th.

DECEMBER   *LEO*

Star-trends prevailing between the 1st and the 22nd will brighten the daily round, and make it possible for you to reorganize your working life on a more stream-lined, productive basis. Any disputes or disharmony will be amicably settled, awkward individuals will be easier to handle, and you can look forward to receiving a pat on the back and a bonus or gift which will help to swell your bank balance.

Lots of stimulating, enjoyable happenings will be centred around hearth and home, especially in the first fortnight. Preparations for the seasonal revelry will occupy much of your time and attention – and you'll be kept busy, too, with phone calls, correspondence, and people who drop in to see you, loaded with interesting news and delicious Christmas goodies!

In the midst of all this hectic activity you'll also contrive somehow to devote some time to yourself, with your health, your appearance and your wardrobe high on the agenda.

Many members of your sign won't wait until the New Year to make their good resolutions, which will demand willpower and determination. You may, for example, decide right now to break certain harmful habits, or go on a diet which will enable you to cut a more dashing figure during the Yuletide festivities.

Courtship, marriage and partnerships' are brilliantly starred from the 23rd onwards. Existing ties will be strengthened, and those who are alone have an excellent chance of finding the single-minded devotion they long for.

Fun, frolic and romantic thrills are forecast, particularly on the 27th. This also promises to be a wonderfully fortunate date for signing contracts and binding agreements. An older person may be instrumental in making one of your cherished aims come true on the 30th.